Our
GOVERNMENT
LEADERS

# VICE PRESIDENT

by Jacqueline Laks Gorman

Reading consultant: Susan Nations, M.Ed., author/literacy coach/consultant

WR WEEKLY READER
EARLY LEARNING LIBRARY

Please visit our web site at: www.earlyliteracy.cc
For a free color catalog describing Weekly Reader® Early Learning Library's
list of high-quality books, call 1-877-445-5824 (USA) or 1-800-387-3178 (Canada).
Weekly Reader® Early Learning Library's fax: (414) 336-0164.

**Library of Congress Cataloging-in-Publication Data**

Gorman, Jacqueline Laks, 1955-
    Vice president / by Jacqueline Laks Gorman.
       p. cm. — (Our government leaders)
    Includes bibliographical references and index.
    ISBN 0-8368-4572-2 (lib. bdg.)
    ISBN 0-8368-4579-X (softcover)
    1. Vice-Presidents—United States—Juvenile literature.  I. Title.  II. Series.
    JK609.5.G67   2005
    352.23'9'0973—dc22                                    2004043128

This edition first published in 2005 by
**Weekly Reader® Early Learning Library**
330 West Olive Street, Suite 100
Milwaukee, WI  53212  USA

Copyright © 2005 by Weekly Reader® Early Learning Library

Editor:  Barbara Kiely Miller
Cover and layout design:  Melissa Valuch
Photo research:  Diane Laska-Swanke

Photo credits:  Cover, title, © Mannie Garcia/Getty Images; p. 5 © Alex Wong/Getty Images; p. 6 © Ed
Clark/Time & Life Pictures/Getty Images; p. 7 © Tim Sloan/AFP/Getty Images; p. 9 © Diana Walker/Time
& Life Pictures/Getty Images; p. 10 © Bob Gomel/Time & Life Pictures; p. 11 © Carl Mydans/Time & Life
Pictures/Getty Images; p. 13 © Paul J. Richards/AFP/Getty Images; p. 14 © Pool Photo/Getty Images;
p. 15 © Dirck Halstead/Time & Life Pictures/Getty Images; p. 17 © North Wind Picture Archives; p. 18
Lyndon B. Johnson Library Photo by Cecil Stoughton; p. 19 © Thomas D. Mcavoy/Time & Life Pictures/
Getty Images; p. 20 © Stock Montage, Inc.; p. 21 © Hulton Archive/Getty Images

Printed in the United States of America

1 2 3 4 5 6 7 8 9 09 08 07 06 05

Cover Photo:  Dick Cheney was elected vice president of the United States in 2000.

# TABLE OF CONTENTS

CHAPTER 1

## Who Is the Vice President?

The vice president of the United States is an important leader. The vice president helps the president in many ways. He gives advice to the president. He helps the president decide the best way to run the country.

The vice president has other duties, or jobs, too. The vice president's job was not always powerful. The job has become more important over the years.

In 2004, Dick Cheney was elected vice president a second time. With his wife Lynne and their grandchildren, he thanked the people who helped him win.

President Dwight D. Eisenhower (*left*) often met with his vice president, Richard Nixon (*right*). They were in office from 1953 to 1961. Nixon became president in 1968.

The vice president and his family live in Washington, D.C. Their house is on the grounds of the U.S. Naval Observatory. The vice president works in the White House. His office is near the president's office.

Trained people protect the vice president and his family. These guards are called the **Secret Service**.

The vice president is paid well to do his job. He travels on a plane called *Air Force Two*.

Secret Service agents must stay close to the vice president. Agents who guarded Vice President Al Gore (*left*) sometimes had to run to keep up with him.

CHAPTER 2

# What Does the Vice President Do?

The law gives the vice president only two duties. The first duty is the most important. The president might not be able to finish his job. He could become sick or die. Then the vice president takes over. Nine vice presidents have had to take over as president. The vice president must be ready for the top job.

The vice president's second duty is important, too. The Senate is part of Congress. **Congress** is the group that makes the country's laws. The vice president is in charge of running the meetings of the Senate. The vice president does not usually vote in the Senate. He only votes if the vote is tied.

As vice president, Dan Quayle (*second from right*) listened when President George H. W. Bush addressed Congress.

Lyndon Johnson (*fourth on the left*) attended many cabinet meetings as vice president. He served under President John Kennedy (*fourth on the right*).

The vice president is a member of the president's cabinet. The **cabinet** is a group of people who are the president's top helpers. Cabinet members run fifteen government departments. The vice president goes to cabinet meetings. They talk about how to fix problems.

The president also asks the vice president to do other things. Sometimes, the vice president leads groups that study problems. The groups try to find answers to the problems. The vice president travels around the world to meet with other leaders, too.

Vice President Henry Wallace made many trips to visit people around the world. He was in office for four years.

CHAPTER 3

## How Does a Person Get to Be Vice President?

The vice president must be at least thirty-five years old. He or she must have been born in the United States. He or she must be a citizen. The vice president and the president are elected together. They are a team. People vote for them together. Their terms are four years long.

Many people have the same ideas about running the country. They belong to groups called **political parties**. The two main political parties hold big meetings, or **conventions**. At the conventions, the parties pick the people, or **candidates**, that they want to be the president and vice president.

John Kerry (*left*) and John Edwards (*right*) were candidates for president and vice president in 2004.

Dick Cheney (*left*) and Joseph Lieberman (*right*) had a debate when they were running for vice president in 2000.

The candidates travel across the country. They talk to voters and give speeches. They have debates with each other about important issues. Election Day is in November. People all over the country vote. The candidates with the most votes are elected president and vice president.

People do not always elect the vice president. Sometimes, the vice president leaves the job. The law says that the president can then name a new vice president.

President Gerald Ford (*right*) chose Nelson Rockefeller (*left*) to be his vice president in 1974.

CHAPTER 4

# Famous Vice Presidents

Many vice presidents did not do great things. They are hard to remember. Other vice presidents were great men. They did good things for the country. A woman has not become vice president yet.

In 1789, John Adams became the first vice president. He thought the vice president's job was dull. He tried to make it more important. Adams was vice president until 1797. Then he was elected president.

© North Wind Picture Archives

John Adams was the United States' first vice president. He served under George Washington for just over eight years.

Vice President Lyndon Johnson was sworn in as the new president after John Kennedy was killed in 1963.

Many vice presidents also wanted to be president. They ran in elections and won.

Others became president after the president died or quit. In 1841, President William Harrison died. John Tyler was the vice president. He was the first vice president to take over after a president died.

Harry Truman was the vice president in 1945.
The United States was fighting World War II.
President Franklin D. Roosevelt died. Truman
became the new president. He worked very
hard to help the country win the war. Truman
ran for president in the next election and won.

Vice President Harry Truman (*left*) became president
after Franklin D. Roosevelt (*right*) died in 1945.

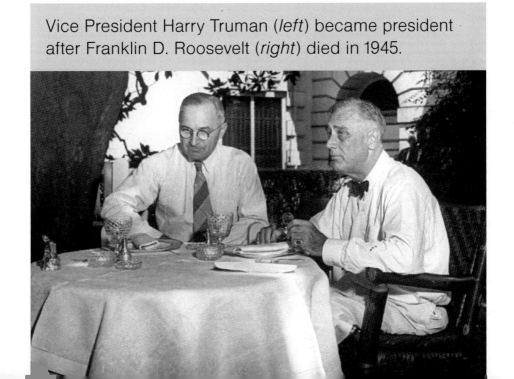

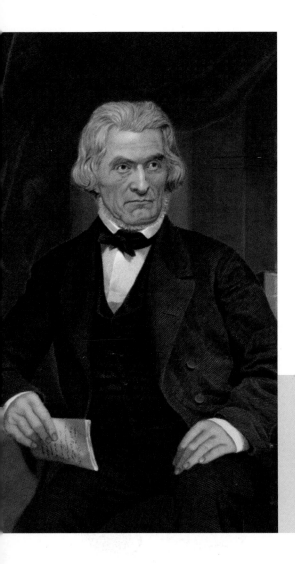

Some fine vice presidents never became president. Walter Mondale was vice president under President Jimmy Carter. Al Gore was vice president under President Bill Clinton. Mondale and Gore both worked hard. Both of them ran for president. Both of them lost.

John C. Calhoun was vice president from 1825 to 1832. He was the vice president under both President John Quincy Adams and President Andrew Jackson.

One vice president is famous for doing the wrong thing. Aaron Burr became vice president in 1801. He argued with Alexander Hamilton, an important man who helped to shape the country. Burr and Hamilton had a duel. Burr killed Hamilton but did not go to jail. He finished his job as vice president.

Vice President Aaron Burr shot and killed Alexander Hamilton in a duel in 1804.

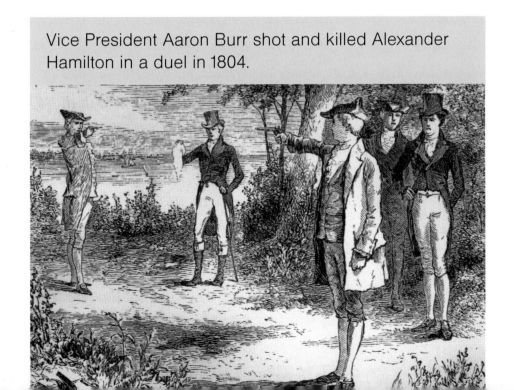

# Glossary

**candidates** — people who seek or are selected by others for an office or honor

**citizen** — an official member of a country who is given certain rights, such as voting and freedom of speech. A citizen also has duties, such as paying taxes.

**debates** — discussions of people's different ideas and why they are for or against something

**duel** — a fight with specific rules between two people who use guns or swords

**political parties** — groups that seek to gain power in the government by picking people to run for office and be elected

**Senate** — one of the two parts of Congress

**U.S. Naval Observatory** — a scientific agency in Washington, D.C. The vice president's official house is on its grounds.

# For More Information

## Books

*How the U.S. Government Works.* Syl Sobel, Pam Tanzey (Barron's Educational Services)

*The Vice Presidency.* Your Government: How It Works (series). (Chelsea House)

*The Vice President of the United States.* America's Leaders (series). Scott Ingram (Blackbirch Press)

## Web Sites

**Ben's Guide to U.S. Government for Kids**
*bensguide.gpo.gov*
A guide to the national government, including the vice presidency

**Children's Biography of the Vice President**
*www.whitehouse.gov/kids/vicepresident*
A guide to the national government, including the vice president and a video tour of his office

# INDEX

## ABOUT THE AUTHOR

**Jacqueline Laks Gorman** is a writer and editor. She grew up in New York City. She has worked on many kinds of books and has written several children's series. She lives with her husband, David, and children, Colin and Caitlin, in DeKalb, Illinois. She always votes in every election.